HMH | into Reading™

my Book 1

Authors and Advisors

Alma Flor Ada • Kylene Beers • F. Isabel Campoy
Joyce Armstrong Carroll • Nathan Clemens
Anne Cunningham • Martha C. Hougen
Elena Izquierdo • Carol Jago • Erik Palmer
Robert E. Probst • Shane Templeton • Julie Washington

Contributing Consultants

David Dockterman • Mindset Works®
Jill Eggleton

MODULE 1

Be a Super Citizen

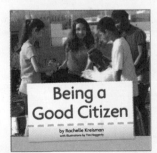

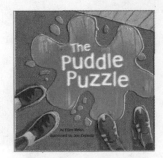

Be a Super Citizen

"You've got to give more than you take."

—Christopher Reeve

How can being a good citizen make a difference to others?

Get Curious Video

Words About Citizenship

Complete the Vocabulary Network to show what you know about the words.

citizen

Meaning: A **citizen** is a member of a community, state, or country.

Synonyms and Antonyms	Drawing

difference

Meaning: When people make a **difference**, they do something that helps others.

Synonyms and Antonyms	Drawing

kind

Meaning: Someone who is **kind** is nice, caring, or gentle.

Synonyms and Antonyms	Drawing

We Are ★ SUPER CITIZENS ★

My dog Bailey is the best! When we learned about good citizens in school, my teacher asked us to think of ways we could be good citizens. I thought about Bailey. She's friendly and gentle. I just knew she could be a good therapy dog.

First, I found a dog club near where I live. My mom and I took Bailey there. Bailey took a test to see how she behaved. She was calm and acted well with strangers. She listened to commands.

After some training classes, we became a therapy dog team. Now my mom and I take Bailey to visit people. Bailey gives them comfort and love.

I like raising a therapy dog. We are good citizens together. Bailey makes a difference in the lives of the people we visit. She helps make their lives better.

FACT

Therapy dogs are not the same as service dogs. Service dogs are trained to provide a certain kind of help for a person with special needs.

Prepare to Read

GENRE STUDY **Fantasies** are stories with made-up events that could not really happen. As you read *Clark the Shark,* look for:

- animal characters who talk and act like people
- the beginning, middle, and end of the story
- how pictures and words help you understand what happens

SET A PURPOSE **Ask questions** before, during, and after you read to help you get information or understand the text. Look for evidence in the text and pictures to answer your questions.

POWER WORDS

munch

bellowed

rough

handle

cool

bounce

grinned

might

Meet Bruce Hale.

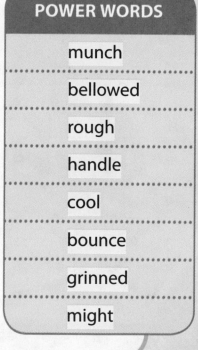

CLARK THE SHARK

by Bruce Hale

illustrated by Guy Francis

In all the wide blue seas, in all the wide blue world,
the top school for fish was Theodore Roosterfish Elementary.
And of all the fish at Theodore Roosterfish, the biggest and
the strongest was Clark the Shark.

Clark loved school, and he loved his teacher, Mrs. Inkydink. He loved to play upsy-downsy and spinna-ma-jig with his friends. Clark *loved* his life.

"SCHOOL IS AWESOME!" shouted Clark the Shark. "Less shouting, more reading," said Mrs. Inkydink.

18

"LUNCHTIME IS SWEEEEET!"

yelled Clark the Shark.

"Munch your *own* lunch," said his best

friend, Joey Mackerel.

"RECESS ROCKS!" bellowed Clark the Shark.

"You are playing rough, Clark!"

19

Yes, Clark loved his life with all of his sharky heart. But he loved everything *way* too much.

He was too loud.

He was too wild.

He was just too much shark for the other fish to handle.

After a while, no one would play with Clark. No one ate lunch with him. No one sat with him at circle time. Even his best friend, Joey Mackerel, said, "Cool your jets, Clark! You're making me crazy!"

One day, Clark asked Mrs. Inkydink, "What's *wrong* with everyone?"

Mrs. Inkydink patted his fin. "Clark, sometimes you play too hard, you munch too hard, and—gosh—you even help too hard."

"But life is SO exciting!" said Clark.

"There's a time and a place for everything," said Mrs. Inkydink. "And sometimes the rule is *stay cool.*"

STAY COOL!

At recess, Clark tried to stay cool, but he pushed the swing with too much zing! "Sorry," said Clark. "I forgot."

"Yikes!" cried Joey Mackerel.

At lunch, Clark tried to stay cool, but everything smelled so good that he munched a bunch of lunches.

"Sorry," said Clark. "I forgot."

"We're STARVING!" said his friends.

In class, Clark tried to stay cool, but a good book got him all shook up.

"Now, Clark!" said Mrs. Inkydink. "This isn't the time or the place. Tell me, what's the rule?"

"Stay cool," said Clark.

"Hey, that rhymes!" he cried.

Then Clark got a big idea in his sharky head. *Maybe if I make a rhyme, I'll remember every time!* he thought. The next day, he put his plan to work.

In class, when lessons got exciting, Clark wanted to bounce up out of his seat.

Instead, he told himself: "When teacher's talking, don't go walking."

And what do you know? It worked!

"Attaboy, Clark!" said Mrs. Inkydink.

Clark smiled. "Lessons are fun!"

At lunch, everything smelled *sooo* yummy. When Clark wanted to eat

and eat and never stop, he told himself: "Only munch your own lunch."

And it worked again!

"Way to go, Clark!" said his friends.

Clark grinned. "Lunch is fun."

At playtime, Clark told himself: "Easy does it, that's the way.

"Then my friends will let me play."

And playtime was fun. Once more, Clark loved his life.

But then a shadow fell across the playground—a *gi-normous* shadow with tentacles galore. "It's a new kid, and he looks scary!" cried Joey Mackerel. "Swim for your lives!"

The squid squashed the slide, and it snapped off the swings.

"Oops. My bad," said the new kid.

"Wait," said Clark. "He just wants to play. Let's find a way!"

And he swam at the new kid with all his might. Clark played harder than he ever had before—upsy-downsy and spinna-ma-jig.

Why, he even made up a new game: tail-whump-a-lumpus!

28

"Wow, that was fun," said the new kid breathlessly, and he settled down.

"If you want to come to school, you've got to stay cool," said Clark.

"That's right, Clark," said Mrs. Inkydink. "And thanks for taking care of our new classmate, Sid the Squid."

"Hooray for Clark the Shark!" everyone cheered.

30

That night Clark's mother asked, "What did you learn at school, dear?"
"There's a time and a place for everything," Clark said. "Sometimes you stay cool."

"But sometimes a shark's gotta do what a shark's gotta do."

Use details from *Clark the Shark* to answer these questions with a partner.

1. **Ask and Answer Questions** What questions did you ask yourself about Clark before, during, and after reading? How did your questions help you understand the story?

2. Why do Clark's friends stop playing with him? How do you think that makes him feel? Use details in the text and pictures to explain your ideas.

3. Choose one of Clark's rhyming rules. Explain how it helps him to be a good citizen.

Talking Tip

Your ideas are important! Be sure to speak loudly and clearly as you share them.

Write a Description

PROMPT How do you know that Clark wants to do the right thing? Use details from the words and pictures to explain your ideas.

PLAN First, think about the story. Then draw a scene that shows Clark trying to do the right thing.

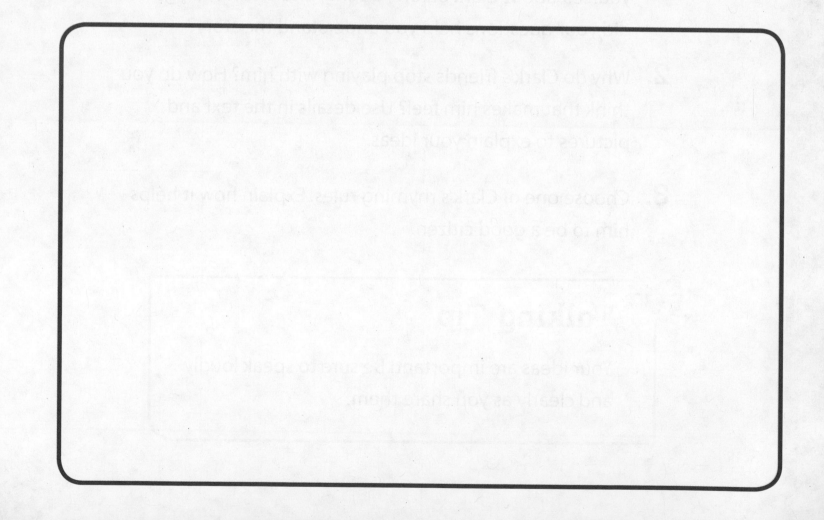

WRITE Now, write sentences to describe a time when Clark tries to do the right thing. Remember to:

- Find details in the story that explain your idea.

- Use describing words to tell what Clark does or tries to do.

_____

_____

_____

_____

_____

_____

_____

_____

_____

_____

Prepare to Read

GENRE STUDY **Fantasies** are stories with made-up events that could not really happen.

MAKE A PREDICTION Preview "A Forest Welcome." Sunny Bunny is moving into a new home. What do you think will happen when she meets her neighbors?

_____

_____

_____

_____

_____

_____

SET A PURPOSE Read to find out what happens when Sunny Bunny moves to her new home.

A Forest Welcome

READ What is the setting of the story? <u>Underline</u> it.

All morning, Sunny Bunny hopped cheerily around the forest. Finally, she stopped near a pretty tree and grinned. She had found the perfect spot to make her new home. *Scritch, scratch.* Sunny's little bunny claws quickly dug at the dirt. A raccoon was resting high up in the tree and heard Sunny Bunny.

"Welcome to the neighborhood," he said. "I am Roy Raccoon, and I am a great digger. Let me help you!" ▶

Close Reading Tip

Put a **?** by the parts you have questions about.

CHECK MY UNDERSTANDING

Why is the setting of the story important?

_____

_____

READ Which animals help Sunny? <u>Underline</u> their names.

Close Reading Tip

Put a ! by a surprising part.

"I am Sunny Bunny," Sunny said to her new friend. "It's nice to meet you, Roy!"

When Barb Bear heard there was a new bunny in town, she threw a big party to welcome Sunny. All the forest animals came. Sunny was thrilled to make so many new friends. When the party ended, it was quite late. Sunny was not sure she could find her way home. Sid Skunk said not to worry because he could see in the dark. He led Sunny all the way home. When she was snug in bed, Sunny smiled. She was going to like her new home!

CHECK MY UNDERSTANDING

What questions did you ask yourself before, during, and after reading? How did your questions help you understand the story?

_____

_____

_____

_____

38

WRITE ABOUT IT Write a short thank-you note from Sunny to one of her new friends. Describe what the character did and how it made Sunny feel. Use details from the story in your answer.

_____

_____

_____

_____

_____

_____

_____

_____

_____

_____

_____

Prepare to Read

GENRE STUDY **Fantasies** are stories with made-up events that could not really happen. As you read *Spoon,* look for:

- characters who are not found in real life
- the setting, or where the story takes place
- a lesson the main character learns

SET A PURPOSE As you read, stop and think if you don't understand something. Reread, ask yourself questions, use what you already know, and look for visual clues to help you understand the text.

POWER WORDS

proper

blue

useful

realize

Meet Amy Krouse Rosenthal.

SPOON

by Amy Krouse Rosenthal   illustrated by Scott Magoon

This is Spoon.

This is Spoon's family.

On Sundays, Spoon goes to visit his Aunt Silver.
He has to be on his very best behavior there.
She's very fancy and proper.

"Good-bye, darling!
Ta, ta!"

At bedtime, Spoon likes to hear the story about his adventurous great-grandmother, who fell in love with a dish and ran off to a distant land.

Lately, though, Spoon had been feeling blue.
"What's wrong?" asked his mother. "You look a bit out of shape."

"Nothing," mumbled Spoon.

"It's just that . . . I don't know . . .
All my friends have it so much better than me.

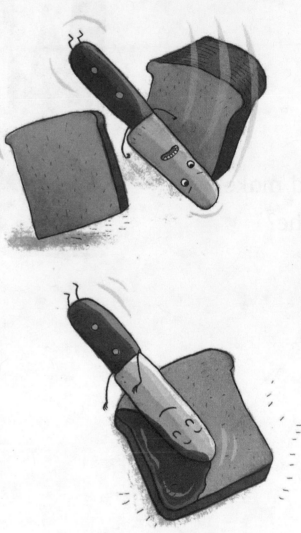

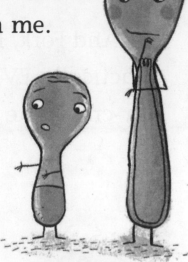

Like Knife.
Knife is so lucky!
He gets to cut,
he gets to spread.
I never get to cut or spread."

"Yes, Knife is pretty spiffy that way, isn't he?"

"And Fork, Fork is so lucky! She gets to go practically EVERYWHERE. I bet she never goes stir-crazy like I do."

"Fork does get out and make herself useful, doesn't she?"

"And Chopsticks! They are so lucky!
Everyone thinks they're really cool and exotic.
No one thinks I'm cool or exotic."

"Those Chopsticks are
something else, aren't they?"

Meanwhile . . . if only Spoon knew what his friends were saying at that very minute!

"Spoon is so lucky!" said Knife. "He's so fun and easygoing. Everyone's so serious with me; no one's ever allowed to be silly with me like they are with Spoon."

"Spoon is so lucky!" said Fork. "He gets to measure stuff. No one ever does that with me."

"Spoon is so lucky!" said Chopsticks. "He can go places by himself. We could never function apart."

That night after bedtime stories, Spoon's mom turned off the light, tucked him in, and said . . .

"You know, Spoon—I wonder if you realize just how lucky you are.

"Your friends will never know
the joy of diving headfirst into
a bowl of ice cream."

"They'll never know what it feels like to clink against the side of a cereal bowl.

"They'll never be able to twirl around in a mug, or relax in a hot cup of tea."

Spoon hadn't thought of it that way before.
He lay awake in bed for a long time. His mind
was racing . . . he felt so alive!

There was only one thing to do.

And so he did.

Turn and Talk

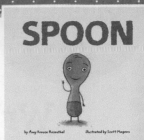

Use details from *Spoon* to answer these questions with a partner.

1. **Monitor and Clarify** What did you do when you came to a part of the text that you didn't understand? Tell how it helped or didn't help you.

2. Which details in the words and pictures help you understand why Spoon feels better at the end of the story?

3. What does this story teach you about being yourself?

Listening Tip

Look at your partner as you listen. Wait until your partner finishes speaking before you talk.

Write an Opinion

PROMPT In your opinion, which character in *Spoon* has the most important job? Look for details in the words and pictures to help you decide.

PLAN First, write which character you chose in the chart. Then write or draw reasons why you chose that character.

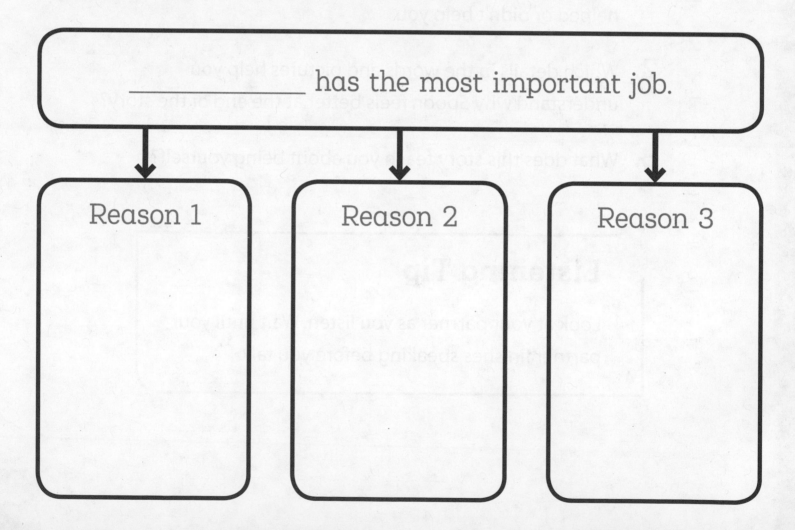

_____ has the most important job.

| Reason 1 | Reason 2 | Reason 3 |

WRITE Now write your opinion about the character you chose. Include reasons that tell why you think that character has the most important job. Remember to:

- Use opinion words like *I believe* or *I think*.

- Use words like *and, because,* and *also* to tell more about your reasons.

_____

_____

_____

_____

_____

_____

_____

_____

_____

Prepare to Read

GENRE STUDY **Fantasies** are stories with made-up events that could not really happen.

MAKE A PREDICTION Preview "Fly Like an Eagle." There is trouble in this nest. You have learned that the setting is an important part of a story. What do you think the setting in this story will be like?

_____

_____

_____

_____

_____

_____

SET A PURPOSE Read to find out what the setting is like and to see if your prediction is right. If not, use what you know about story settings to make a new prediction.

Fly Like an Eagle

READ What do you think *squabbling* means? Use the text and picture for help.

It was a bright, sunny day. High up in a tree, in a big nest, a brother and sister eaglet were squabbling.

"What is the problem here?" asked Mama Eagle.

"He called me a symbol," said Sister Eagle.

"You *are* a symbol," said her brother.

"My little eaglets, you are both symbols," Papa Eagle said. ▶

Close Reading Tip

Mark important words with *.

CHECK MY UNDERSTANDING

Which details from the story tell you it is made up?

_____

_____

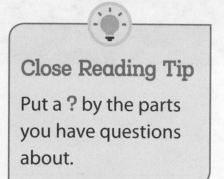

READ As you read, ask yourself questions about parts that don't make sense. Then go back and reread those parts.

Close Reading Tip

Put a **?** by the parts you have questions about.

"Being a symbol is something you can be proud of," Mama Eagle explained. "It means you stand for something."

The two eaglets were confused. They weren't standing. They were sitting!

"Eagles are symbols for this great country of ours," said Papa Eagle. "We are free to fly anywhere we wish. We remind people that they are also free. We are big and strong. We remind people that our country is also big and strong. Being a symbol means we stand for, or represent, something else."

"That's so cool!" said Brother Eagle.

"Wow," Sister Eagle said. "I am proud to be a symbol."

CHECK MY UNDERSTANDING

What is the author's purpose for writing this story?

_____

_____

_____

WRITE ABOUT IT "Fly Like an Eagle" is a fantasy about eagles and why they are important to us. How does the author make it fun to read? Use details from the story in your answer.

_____

_____

_____

_____

_____

_____

_____

_____

_____

_____

_____

Prepare to Read

GENRE STUDY **Informational text** is one kind of nonfiction. It gives facts about a topic. As you read *Being a Good Citizen*, look for:

- main topic and details
- photographs
- facts about events

SET A PURPOSE As you read, **summarize** the text. Use your own words to describe the most important ideas in an order that makes sense.

POWER WORDS

elected

local

mock

compliment

Build Background: Ways to Help Your Community

Being a Good Citizen

by Rachelle Kreisman
with illustrations by Tim Haggerty

Community Living

Everyone is part of a community. A community is a place where people live, work, and play. Each community is made up of neighborhoods. Those neighborhoods are made up of people. You are one of those people! So you are part of a community.

Good citizens make the community a better place. A citizen is a person who lives in a certain place. It can be a town or city, state, or country.

How can you be a good citizen? Make a difference in your community! Learn about your elected officials and follow rules. Get involved in community activities. Be a good neighbor and help others. Do you want to learn more? Of course, you do! Keep reading to find out more about how you can be a good citizen.

JUST JOKING!

Q: How did the ocean greet its neighbor?

A: It waved!

Get Involved

Good citizens are involved in the community. They get to know their neighbors and other citizens. They work to make their community a better place to live.

What can you do to get involved? Start by taking part in after-school activities. Join a community center or youth group. They have programs and activities just for kids. You can have fun and make new friends.

After-school activities can be a good way to try new things.

JUST JOKING!

Q: Did you hear the joke about the community center's roof?

A: Never mind—it's over your head!

Another way to get involved is to follow local news. That will let you know what is going on in your community. For example, you might learn that your police department is teaching a free bike safety class. Maybe you will want to take the class.

How can you follow the news? Read school and local newspapers. Watch the local news with a parent. Then talk about what you learned. Ask family members their opinions and share your own.

Being a good citizen includes voting. Citizens can vote in local, state, and national elections. You must be 18 years old to vote in most states.

Every four years, citizens elect the president of the United States. Kids can vote too! How? Many schools invite kids to take part in a mock election. It helps students learn about the election process.

DID YOU KNOW?
People in the United States vote on Election Day. It is always the Tuesday after the first Monday in November.

How else can you get involved? Learn about your community history. Visit museums and town landmarks. Go with a parent to take a tour of your city hall. Meet some of your elected officials. Attend a school board meeting.

Some schools have a student council. They organize special activities and help make school decisions. If you have a student council, you can vote to elect officers. You may also want to serve on the council!

THE STORY OF TEXAS

TEXAS STATE HISTORY MUSEUM

Most museums welcome students.

Help Others

Good citizens are active in community service. They volunteer their time to help others. They also donate items and money to people in need. That can make a big difference in people's lives.

Helping others can make a difference in your life too. It can bring you a lot of joy! Doing good deeds can inspire others to do the same.

FUN FACT

Doing a kind act can make you just as happy as receiving one. Both affect your brain in the same way. They make your brain give off feel-good chemicals, say scientists.

What can you do to help others? Start by doing random acts of kindness. Those acts are small, kind gestures. For example, draw a picture for a friend or family member. Say a friendly "hello" to a neighbor. Give flowers to a teacher. Hold the door open for the next person. Read a book to a younger child. Give someone a compliment.

You can do random acts of kindness every day. See how many kind acts you can do for others.

Being a good citizen helps make your community a better place. It also makes you feel good about yourself. Are you ready?

Turn and Talk

Being a Good Citizen
by Rochelle Kreisman
with illustrations by Tim Haggerty

Use details from *Being a Good Citizen* to answer these questions with a partner.

1. **Summarize** What have you learned about good citizens from reading this text?

2. Find three questions the author asks readers. Why do you think she asks questions instead of just telling the facts?

3. Use details from the text to tell how helping in the community can also help you.

Talking Tip

Use details from the text to explain your ideas. Complete the sentence below.

I read that _____.

Write Directions

PROMPT If someone asked you for directions about how to be a good citizen, what would you tell him or her? Use details from the words and pictures to explain your ideas.

PLAN First, think of three steps to follow to be a good citizen. Write or draw them below.

Step 1	Step 2	Step 3

WRITE Now write directions that tell how to be a good citizen. Be sure your directions are easy to follow. Remember to:

- Choose the most important details in the text.

- Use action words that tell your readers exactly what to do.

_____

_____

_____

_____

_____

_____

_____

_____

_____

_____

Prepare to Read

GENRE STUDY **Informational text** is nonfiction. It gives facts about a topic.

MAKE A PREDICTION Preview "Be a Good Digital Citizen." You know that informational text has facts. What do you think you will learn from this text?

_____

_____

_____

_____

_____

_____

SET A PURPOSE Read to find out what the author wants you to know about being a good digital citizen.

Be a Good Digital Citizen

READ What are digital citizens? <u>Underline</u> the sentence that tells you.

Every time people go online, they become part of the online community. They might be on social media or sending emails. They might just be surfing the web.

Digital citizens are people who work or play in the online community. Just like in other communities, there are rules that should be followed. ▶

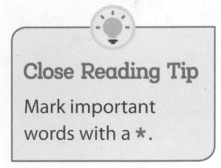

Close Reading Tip

Mark important words with a *.

CHECK MY UNDERSTANDING

What is the author's main purpose for writing this page of text?

_____

_____

_____

READ As you read, think about what rules digital citizens follow. <u>Underline</u> three rules.

Close Reading Tip

Mark important ideas with *.

Children can be digital citizens, too. Some rules help keep children safe. Children should always ask a trusted adult before going online. They should only go to websites that are approved. Children should tell an adult if they see something online that bothers them.

All digital citizens should talk online the way they would talk in person. They should use kind words and be respectful. They should not use words that may hurt someone's feelings.

These rules keep the online community a safe place to work and play!

CHECK MY UNDERSTANDING

Which important ideas from the text would you use in a summary?

_____

_____

_____

WRITE ABOUT IT What other things can you do to be a good
digital citizen? Write two more ideas. Use details from the text in
your answer.

_____

_____

_____

_____

_____

_____

_____

_____

_____

_____

_____

Prepare to Read

GENRE STUDY **Realistic fiction** stories are made up but could happen in real life. As you read *Picture Day Perfection*, look for:

- the beginning, middle, and end of the story
- characters who act and talk like real people
- problems that real people might have
- ways pictures and words help readers understand the story

SET A PURPOSE As you read, **create mental images,** or make pictures in your mind, to help you understand details in the text.

POWER WORDS

planned

perfect

hamper

disaster

scowl

mood

queasy

fiddled

Meet Deborah Diesen.

PICTURE DAY PERFECTION

by Deborah Diesen   illustrated by Dan Santat

I'd planned for months. This was going to be the year of the perfect school picture.

But some days, not everything goes according to plan.

The day started with the worst case of bedhead *ever*.

EXHIBIT A: FRONT VIEW

EXHIBIT C: BACK VIEW

EXHIBIT B: SIDE VIEW

EXHIBIT D: THE LOOK ON MY BROTHER'S FACE WHEN HE SAW MY HAIR.

Then it took me *quite* some time to unearth my favorite shirt. I finally found it at the *very* bottom of the hamper.

You might call it "stained."
You might call it "wrinkled."
You might even call it "smelly."
You wouldn't be wrong.

Breakfast was "Picture Day Pancakes," a family tradition.
This year's festivities involved a small syrup disaster.

More accurately described as a *large* syrup disaster.

And it occurred exactly as the bus pulled up.

I had a feeling we'd be getting a new family tradition.

On the bus, I got into a small bit of trouble.

Make that a *large* bit of trouble. The bus driver made me sit in the seat *right behind him* for the rest of the ride.

By the time I got into school, my picture day face was fixed in a scowl.

In class, Mrs. Smith collected our photo order forms. Do you think my mom checked "Emerald Green" for my photo background? Or "Peacock Blue?" Or "Pizzazzy Purple"?

No. Once again, of all the backgrounds in the world, Mom checked snoring-boring "Traditional Gray."

No one gets "Traditional Gray."

BACKGROUND COLOR
CHOOSE ONE:

Except for me.

And it just so happens to be the only color in
the world that makes my favorite shirt disappear.
All but the stains and the wrinkles.

After that, the teacher had us all stand up and practice our Picture Day smiles. Personally, I thought we needed a little something to get us in the Picture Day mood.

Whoops!
Got myself in trouble.

Again.

Luckily, I got to rejoin the class in time for Art.
Art involved quite a lot of paint.
Or at least it did for *me*.

Finally, it was time to line up for our photos.

Ned, just in front of me, got the *last* complimentary plastic comb.

I watched as classmate after classmate smiled for the camera. I got queasy listening to everyone say "Cheese."

I can't *stand* cheese.

The mere thought of it turns me green! *Deeply* green. And just as my face reached its most *awful* pea-green shade, it was . . . *my turn*.

I stepped forward.
I sat down on the stool.
It was hard as a rock, and cold as an iceberg.

"Just a sec," said the photographer
as he fiddled with the camera knobs.

As I sat and waited, everything that had happened rushed through my mind. The monstrous messes. The muddles and the mix-ups. The whole day, from the moment I'd rolled out of bed, had gone . . .

PERFECTLY!

Even better than planned!
This year, I was finally going to
have *the perfect school picture.*

And that's when I heard a
CLICK!

In a flash, all my hard work—

my perfectly tangled hair,
my perfectly rumpled shirt,
my perfectly sticky face,
my perfectly composed scowl,
that perfect boring background,
those perfect paint splatters,
that perfect sickly pallor—

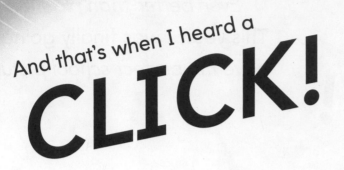

WASTED!

USELESS!

RUINED,

in a moment of weakness,
by an unexpected smile.
Mom says it's my best picture ever.

But just *wait* till she sees *next* year's.

Use details from *Picture Day Perfection* to answer these questions with a partner.

1. **Create Mental Images** What does the boy want his school photo to look like? Use details in the text to help you picture it in your mind. Then describe your picture to a partner.

2. What was the author's purpose for writing this story? Why do you think she called it *Picture Day Perfection?*

3. How is the boy different from characters you've read about recently? Explain whether you think he learns a lesson.

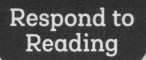

Talking Tip

Complete the sentence to ask your partner for more information about an answer.

Tell me more about _____.

Write a Sequel

PROMPT Use what you know about the boy in *Picture Day Perfection* to write sentences about what he might do on next year's picture day. Look for details in the words and pictures to help you think of ideas.

PLAN First, draw a picture of one thing the boy might try next year. Add a caption to describe what the boy is doing.

WRITE Now write your sequel! Explain what you think the boy's plan will be for next year's picture day. Remember to:

- Look for details in the story that give clues about what the boy might do next year.

- Write details that describe what the boy is thinking, feeling, and hoping.

_____

_____

_____

_____

_____

_____

_____

_____

_____

_____

Prepare to Read

GENRE STUDY **Realistic fiction** stories are made up but could happen in real life.

MAKE A PREDICTION Preview "Picture This!" In this story, a girl comes up with a plan to raise money. What do you think her plan will be?

_____

_____

_____

_____

_____

_____

_____

SET A PURPOSE Read to find out more about the girl and her plan to raise money.

Picture This!

READ Which words help you picture what the yard looks like that Saturday? <u>Underline</u> them.

The local animal shelter needed money. I had a great idea! I could have a car-and-dog wash. Mom and Dad said they would help. It was going to be a lot of work.

"You'll be *sor*-ry!" my older sister sang out.

On Saturday, we were in the front yard surrounded by buckets and hoses. Our sign read *Save the Animal Shelter!* ▶

Close Reading Tip

Mark important ideas with a *****.

CHECK MY UNDERSTANDING

What does the girl's older sister think about the plan?

_____

_____

107

READ How does the girl feel about her day? <u>Underline</u> the words that are clues.

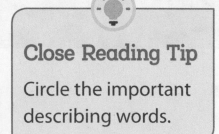

Close Reading Tip

Circle the important describing words.

People started to arrive. The bookstore owner showed up. Then the mail carrier and baker got here. Everyone in town seemed to have a car or dog that needed washing. We were so busy!

Even my sister decided to lend a hand. Some of my friends showed up to help, too! We were all wet and soapy. The dogs and the cars were all sparkling clean, though!

"We should get a picture," someone said. "The shelter would love a picture with all the clean dogs!"

Yes! The day turned out just as I'd hoped!

CHECK MY UNDERSTANDING

Which details help you create a mental picture of the car-and-dog wash?

_____

_____

_____

WRITE ABOUT IT "Picture This!" is a story about a girl who wants to help her community. What kind of person do you think she is? Write a few sentences about her for the town newspaper. Use details from the story in your answer.

_____

_____

_____

_____

_____

_____

_____

_____

_____

_____

_____

Prepare to View

GENRE STUDY **Videos** are short movies that give you information or something for you to watch for enjoyment. As you watch *Get Involved: Be Awesome!*, notice:

- how pictures, sounds, and words work together
- what the video is about
- how the video makes you feel
- what the video is trying to persuade you to do

SET A PURPOSE Think about the video's **central idea.** Can you figure out its message? Think about how that message helps you understand what it means to be a good citizen.

Build Background: Making a Difference

Get Involved:
BE AWESOME!

As You View Are you ready to make your mark? Listen for details about how to become involved in your community. How do the ideas in the video help you understand what it means to be a super citizen?

Use details from *Get Involved: Be Awesome!* to answer these questions with a partner.

1. **Central Idea** What message does the video share? What does the girl try to persuade you to do?

2. What does the girl mean when she says "make your mark"?

3. The girl says to keep trying when things get tough. Do you think that is good advice? Explain why or why not.

Listening Tip

Be sure to wait until your partner has finished speaking before asking a question or adding new information.

Let's Wrap Up!

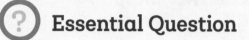 **Essential Question**

How can being a good citizen make a difference to others?

Pick one of these activities to show what you have learned about the topic.

1. The Award Goes to...

You have read about what it means to be a good citizen. Think about someone you know who has made a difference to others. Compare the person to one of the characters you read about. Create a Super Citizen Certificate for that person. Tell a partner whom you chose and why.

2. A Letter to Me

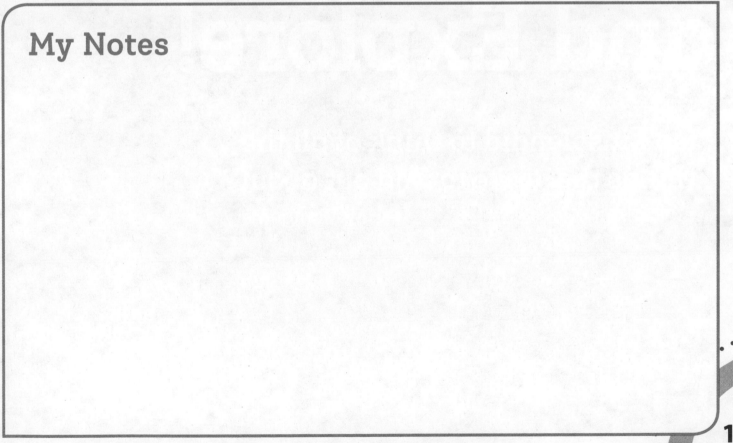

We can all make a difference in our own special way. How will YOU be a good citizen this year? Write a letter to yourself to explain your plan. Think about what you are good at and what you like to do. Look back at the texts for ideas about how to be a good citizen.

Word Challenge

Can you use the word difference in your letter?

My Notes

Look Around and Explore!

"Isn't it splendid to think of all the things there are to find out about?"

—L. M. Montgomery

Essential Question

How does exploring help us understand the world around us?

Video

117

Words About Discovering Our World

Complete the Vocabulary Network to show what you know about the words.

examine

Meaning: When you **examine** something, you look at it carefully.

Synonyms and Antonyms	Drawing

identify

Meaning: When you **identify** something, you say what it is.

Synonyms and Antonyms	Drawing

record

Meaning: When you **record** notes, you write them down.

Synonyms and Antonyms	Drawing

What's the Matter?

Everything around you is made up of matter. There are three kinds of matter: **solid**, **liquid**, and **gas**.

Look around for different kinds of matter right in your classroom. Use the **Kinds of Matter** section to figure out what kind of matter each thing is. Can you find all three kinds of matter?

Which kind of matter did you find the most of?

Kinds of Matter

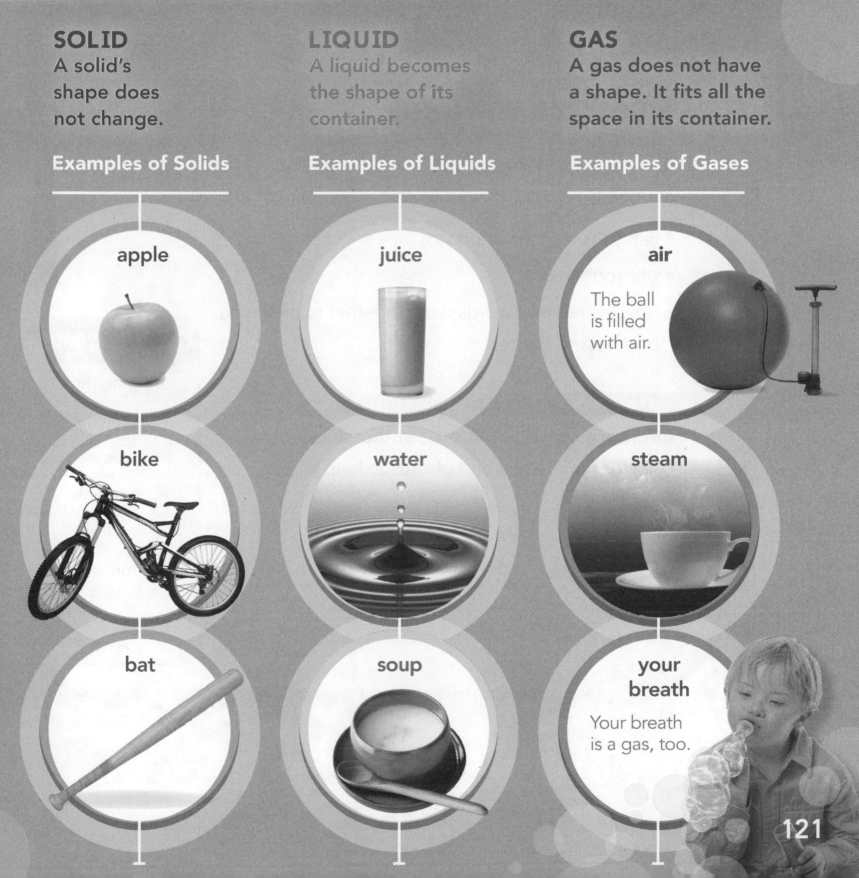

SOLID
A solid's shape does not change.

Examples of Solids

apple

bike

bat

LIQUID
A liquid becomes the shape of its container.

Examples of Liquids

juice

water

soup

GAS
A gas does not have a shape. It fits all the space in its container.

Examples of Gases

air

The ball is filled with air.

steam

your breath

Your breath is a gas, too.

Prepare to Read

GENRE STUDY **Informational text** is nonfiction. It gives facts about a topic. As you read *Many Kinds of Matter*, look for:

- captions with art or photos
- photographs
- how visuals and words work together to help you understand the text

SET A PURPOSE Read to make smart guesses, or **inferences,** about things the author does not say. Use clues in the text and photos to help you.

POWER WORDS

amount

material

space

example

easily

forms

planet

tasty

Build Background: Solids, Liquids, and Gases

MANY KINDS OF MATTER

by Jennifer Boothroyd

MATTER

Matter is everywhere. Matter is anything that has mass and volume. Mass is the amount of material in an object. Volume is the amount of space an object takes up.

Trees, lakes, and people are matter. All have mass and volume.

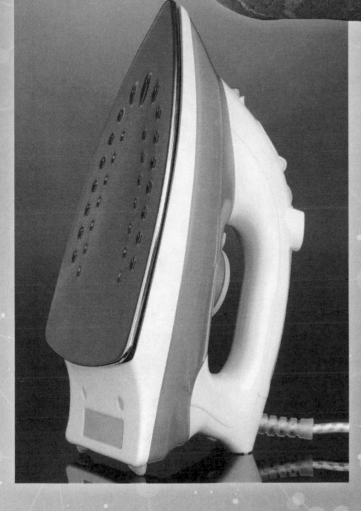

There are three kinds of matter.

The three kinds of matter are solids, liquids, and gases.

SOLIDS

Books, rocks, and toys are solids.

Solid matter holds its own shape. Solids do not take the shape of their container. Marbles fill a jar. But the marbles are still round.

Books are one **example** of a solid.

The shape of solids does not change when you put them in a container.

Solids are not easy to compress. *Compress* means to squeeze something into a tight space. Bottles and cans are solids. It's not easy to squeeze them into this recycling bin!

Solids do not flow.
Solid candies don't spread
across ice cream the way
hot fudge sauce does.

Candy sprinkles
are solids. They
do not flow over
ice cream.

LIQUIDS

Oil, syrup, and water are liquids.

Liquid matter does not hold its own shape. Liquids take the shape of their container. Water inside a swimming pool takes on the shape of the pool.

Oil is one example of a liquid.

Water in a square pool takes on a square shape.

Liquids are not easy to compress. Milk is a liquid. You couldn't fit the milk in the jug into the little carton.

Liquids flow. Liquid syrup spreads across pancakes.

GASES

Air, steam, and your breath are gases.

Your breath is one example of a gas.

Gas matter does not hold its own shape. Gases take the shape of their container. The air inside a hot air balloon takes on the shape of the balloon.

Gases are easy to compress. Carbon dioxide is a gas. It's inside soda cans. It's squeezed into the cans to give the soda bubbles.

Carbon dioxide rushes out of soda cans when you open them.

Gases flow. The air inside a bubble spreads to fill the space inside the bubble.

MATTER AND CHANGES

Matter can change from one kind to another.

Some solids can change to liquids. Some liquids can change to gases.

Water is a special kind of matter. You know that water is a liquid. But it can easily be found in all three forms on our planet.

The liquid in this cup is changing to a gas.

Water becomes a solid if it is cooled.

It turns into ice.

Water turns into ice when it freezes. Water freezes when it reaches a temperature of 32°F (0°C).

Water becomes a gas if it is heated.

It turns into steam.

Water turns into steam when it boils. Water boils when it reaches a temperature of 212°F (100°C).

Water at any temperature can change into water vapor. Water vapor is a gas.

This change is called evaporation.

Some people use a drying rack after washing their dishes. The dishes dry after the water evaporates.

Water vapor changes back into liquid water when it cools in the air.

This change is called condensation.

You can see condensation after a hot shower. The water vapor touches the shower door and turns back into a liquid.

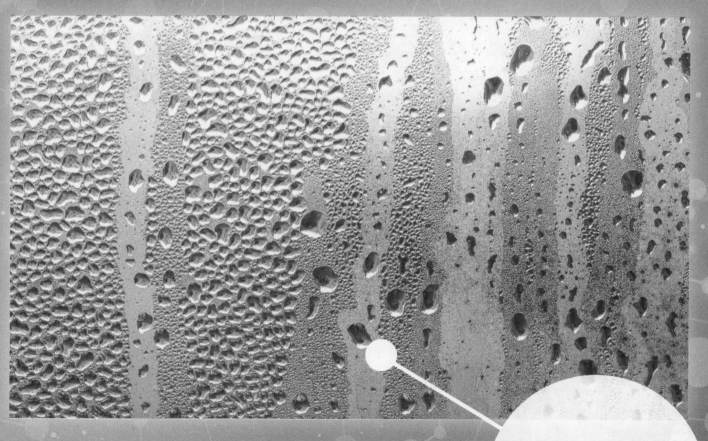

Have you ever seen condensation on a shower door?

Other matter can change forms, too. Cheese is a solid. It melts when it gets hot. It changes to a liquid.

Bread dipped in melted cheese is a **tasty** treat.

Juice is a liquid. It freezes when it gets cold. It changes to a solid.

Ice pops can be made by freezing juice.

We use solids, liquids, and gases every day.

They are an important part of our lives and our planet.

Use details from *Many Kinds of Matter* to answer these questions with a partner.

1. **Make Inferences** Look at the cup on page 134. What is causing the liquid in that cup to change to a gas? How do you know?

2. Compare the three kinds of matter. How are solids, liquids, and gases the same? How are they different?

3. What examples does the text give for each kind of matter? What other examples can you name?

Listening Tip

Listen politely to your partner, and wait until it is your turn to speak.

Write a Description

PROMPT How does a snowman change as it melts? Use details from the words and pictures in *Many Kinds of Matter* to explain your ideas.

PLAN First, picture a snowman in your mind and write words that describe it. Then, picture a melted snowman and write words that describe it.

Snowman	Melted Snowman

WRITE Now, write sentences to describe how a snowman changes as it melts. Remember to:

- Find details in the text and pictures that tell about how matter can change.

- Use describing words.

_____

_____

_____

_____

_____

_____

_____

_____

_____

_____

Prepare to Read

Informational text is nonfiction. It gives facts about a topic.

Preview "Are You Curious?" Our world is full of things that make us wonder and feel curious. What do you think you will read about?

_____

_____

_____

_____

_____

_____

Read to make inferences about people who are curious.

Are You Curious?

READ Which words help you understand what *curious* means? <u>Underline</u> them.

Being curious means wondering about things. It means being excited to explore. When we are curious, we ask questions. We might ask questions about how something works or why things happen. We can observe things we are curious about. This helps us find answers. Those answers can surprise us. They might even make us more curious! ▶

Close Reading Tip

Mark important ideas with a *.

CHECK MY UNDERSTANDING

How do people find answers when they are curious?

_____

_____

_____

READ Which sentences help you understand how being curious can lead to making discoveries? <u>Underline</u> them.

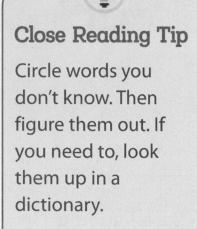

Close Reading Tip

Circle words you don't know. Then figure them out. If you need to, look them up in a dictionary.

Curiosity leads to learning and new, exciting discoveries. Long ago, people asked, "Why can birds fly?" They watched birds in the sky. They discovered that a bird's wing shape was one reason why it could fly. Eventually, what people had learned about a bird's wings was used to build the airplane.

We know a lot about the world around us because people were curious. And there are always more questions we can ask! Never be afraid to say, "I don't know." That will help your curiosity grow. We can only learn what we don't know.

What do you wonder about?

CHECK MY UNDERSTANDING

What can you infer from the text about people who are curious?

_____

_____

_____

_____

WRITE ABOUT IT What makes you a curious person? Use details from the text in your answer. Try to include the words *wonder, discovery,* and *curious.*

_____

_____

_____

_____

_____

_____

_____

_____

_____

_____

_____

Prepare to Read

GENRE STUDY **Fantasies** are stories with made-up events that could not really happen. As you read *The Great Fuzz Frenzy*, look for:

- animal characters that talk and act like people
- the beginning, middle, and ending of the story
- setting, or where the story takes place

SET A PURPOSE As you read, **make connections** by finding ways that this text is like things in your life and other texts you have read. This will help you understand and remember the text.

POWER WORDS

gasped

frenzy

battleground

feud

Meet Janet Stevens and Susan Stevens Crummel.

by Janet Stevens and Susan Stevens Crummel

illustrated by Janet Stevens

THE GREAT FUZZ FRENZY

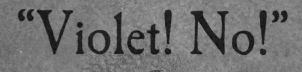

"Violet! No!"

"Violet! Where's the ball?"

"WOOF!"

150

Down it went.

BOINK!
BOINK!

"Run for your life!"

"Watch out below!"

THUMP!
THUMP!

RUMBLE!
RUMBLE!

"HELP! HELP!"
"HEEELLLP!"

PLUNK.

There it sat—perfectly still.
The prairie dogs waited—perfectly still.

Slowly they crept out.

Inch by inch. Dog by dog.

"What is it?"

"A thing."

"A good thing or a bad thing?"

"A round thing."

"A strange thing."

"A scary thing."

"What should we do?"

"Don't touch it!"

"Is it alive?"

"Ssshhh!"

"Stand back!" boomed a voice. "You act like gutless groundhogs—afraid of your own shadow!"

"Oh no, it's Big Bark!"

"Big *Mouth* is more like it."

"He's the meanest dog around."

"I thought he left town."

"Well, I'm back," growled Big Bark. "So out of my way. Let me have a look."

But before anyone could move, little Pip Squeak raced past
Big Bark, reached out, and poked the big round thing.

"Noooooo!" the crowd yelled.

"It's fuzzy!" said Pip.

"Oooooooh!" the crowd gasped.

A tiny piece of fuzz was caught in Pip's claw.
She looked at it. Turned it. Sniffed it. Then she
put it on her head. "Look at me!"

"Ahhhhhh!" the crowd sighed.

"Quit hammin' it up, you half-pint hamster!"
snarled Big Bark. *"I'm* in charge."

But those prairie dogs didn't listen. They had to have fuzz.

"I like it."
"Me, too."
"I want some."
"Do you?"

"Oh yes!"
"So do I!"
"So do we!"
"So do they!"

"Big Bark, move over!"
"Get out of our way!"

They charged past him
and grabbed at the fuzz.

The prairie dogs pulled it. Puffed it.
Stretched it. Fluffed it.
Tugged it. Twirled it.
Spiked it. Swirled it.
They fuzzed their ears, their heads, their noses.
They fuzzed their feet, their tails, their toeses.

Big Bark was beside himself. "Listen to me, you ridiculous rodents! Stop this fuzzy foolishness!"

But those prairie dogs didn't listen.
They were busy being hot dogs and silly dogs.
Corny dogs and frilly dogs.
Top dogs. Funny dogs.
Superdogs. Bunny dogs.

"You're all nuts, you
squirrelly fuzz freaks!"
yelled Big Bark, storming off.

News of the fuzz spread from hole to hole. Burrow to burrow. Town to town.

Soon prairie dogs from everywhere were coming to see that fuzz.

They came, they saw, they picked.

They twisted it. Braided it. Danced, and paraded it.

It was a fuzz frenzy.

A fuzz fiesta.

A fuzz fandangle.

The whole prairie was abuzz about fuzz.

They picked and pruned and pulled and pinched.
They pinched and pulled and pruned and picked.

Until . . .
the fuzz ran out.

That big round thing was fuzzless. Naked as a plucked chicken.

Some prairie dogs got a lot of fuzz.
Some got a little. Some got no fuzz
at all—and they were mad.

"Give me that fuzz!"
"Why?"

"Because."
"It's my fuzz."
"Well, it *was!*"

"Get that fuzz!"

"GET THAT
FUZZ!"

Pulling, grabbing, swiping, nabbing, poking, jabbing—it was war! War between the fuzzes and the fuzz-nots. Their peaceful town was a **battleground**. It was a fuzz fight.

A fuzz **feud**.

A fuzz fiasco.

"I started this," moaned Pip Squeak. "I have to do something. Everyone! Stop! Stop fighting!"

But those prairie dogs didn't listen. The battle raged on—friend against friend, cousin against cousin, dog against dog—until no one was left standing.

They were pooped. Fuzzled out. Fast asleep.

Hours later the prairie dogs began to stir.

"Uh-oh!"

"Where's the fuzz?"

"I don't know!"

"Where did it go?"

"SOMEONE HAS STOLEN OUR FUZZ!"
cried Pip Squeak.

171

"I DID!" barked a voice
from above.

"I STOLE THE FUZZ!"

The prairie dogs froze. Then they raced up,
up, up the long tunnel. There stood Big Bark,
covered with fuzz from head to tail.

"I'm king of the fuzz!" he snarled. "Do you
hear me? I'm king of the—"

SWOOP!

The sky went black.

"What happened?"

"Where's Big Bark?"

"Look!"

There he was, high above their heads, dangling from the talons of an eagle.

"No more Big Bark!" the crowd cheered. "Yaaaaaay!"

"Don't *yaaaaaay*! He's one of *us*!" yelled Pip. "We have to save him! How would *you* like to be Eagle's lunch?"

"Noooooo!" the crowd yelled.

"Big Bark, wiggle free!" the prairie dogs shouted.

"Shake loose!"

"Hurry!"

"We"ll catch you!"

Big Bark twisted and turned, wormed and squirmed. At last he was free of the fuzz!

"Yaaaaaay!" the crowd cheered.

Big Bark fell faster and faster.
"Noooooo!" Prairie dogs scattered.

"Get back here!" yelled Pip. "Quick!
Make a circle! Hold out your paws!"
They ran left, then right, then left.

PLOP!

"You saved me!" Big Bark cried. "But I stole your fuzz! Now it's gone forever."

"Good," said Pip Squeak. "Fuzz is *trouble*. Right?"

"Yaaaaaay!" the crowd cheered. Friend hugged friend. Cousin hugged cousin. Dog hugged dog.

"We don't need fuzz," said Pip. "But with Eagle around, we do need a watchdog with a big—"

"BAAARRRK!" Big Bark rose up on his hind legs. "Eagle's back! BAAARRRK! This is not a test! BAAARRRK! All dogs below! BAAARRRK!"

The prairie dogs raced down, down, down the long tunnel.

179

"Whew! We made it!"

"That was close!"

"Three cheers for Big Bark, the best watchdog ever!"

"YIP, YIP, YAAAAAAY! YIP, YIP, YAAAAAAY! YIP, YIP, YAAAAAAY!"

"Just doing my job!" Big Bark smiled.

"Are we ever getting tangled up with fuzz again?" cried Pip Squeak.

"Noooooo!" the crowd yelled. "No more fuzz! No more fuzz!"

And from that day forward, the prairie dogs lived happily—and fuzzlessly—ever after.

Use details from *The Great Fuzz Frenzy* to answer these questions with a partner.

1. Make Connections Think about a time when it was hard for you to share. How does that help you understand what happens when the prairie dogs find the fuzz?

2. Why do the prairie dogs cheer when Eagle takes Big Bark? Why do their feelings change?

3. Find places in the story where the authors repeat words and sounds. How does this make the story fun to read?

Talking Tip

Ask to learn more about one of your partner's ideas. Complete the sentence below.

Tell me more about _____.

Write an Invitation

PROMPT The prairie dogs have a celebration after they find the tennis ball. What could they say to persuade other prairie dogs to join in the fun? Use details from the words and pictures to explain your ideas.

PLAN First, think of reasons why other prairie dogs would want to join the celebration. Write or draw them below.

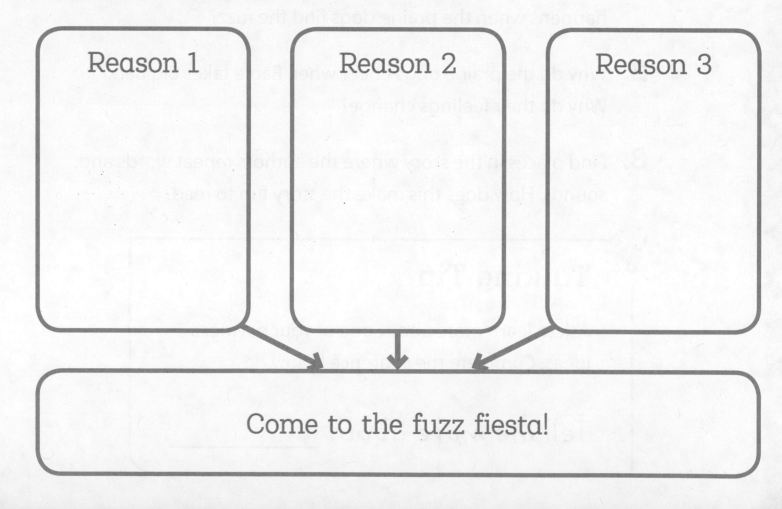

Reason 1

Reason 2

Reason 3

Come to the fuzz fiesta!

WRITE Now, write sentences to invite the prairie dogs to the fuzz fiesta. Remember to:

- Look for details in the story that show how the prairie dogs feel about fuzz.

- Describe the celebration in a way that will make other prairie dogs excited about going.

_____

_____

_____

_____

_____

_____

_____

_____

Prepare to Read

GENRE STUDY **Fantasies** are stories with made-up events that could not really happen.

MAKE A PREDICTION Preview "Bear Up There." Grandpa, Billie Bear, and Honeysuckle are lost in the woods. You know that a fantasy has make-believe events. What do you think will happen?

_____

_____

_____

_____

_____

_____

_____

SET A PURPOSE Read to find out what happens to the bears when it gets dark outside.

Bear Up There

"Grandpa, we're lost!" Billie Bear's cry cut through the Great Wood. Her twin, Honeysuckle, opened her eyes wide.

The cubs loved hiking with Grandpa. He never told them to hurry. He liked to move slowly. Today they had picked lots of blueberries. They had splashed in a river and fished for salmon. Now it was getting dark, and they were lost. ▶

Close Reading Tip

Write **C** when you make a connection.

CHECK MY UNDERSTANDING

How does the illustration help you understand what Grandpa is like?

_____

_____

_____

185

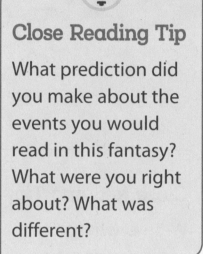

Close Reading Tip

What prediction did you make about the events you would read in this fantasy? What were you right about? What was different?

"A bear is never lost," Grandpa said with a wink. "The Great Bear will take us home." Grandpa's paw traced the outline of a huge bear in the stars. "That bear up there is Ursa Major. *Ursa* means bear, and *major* means big."

"There IS a bear up there!" Honeysuckle cried out.

"There are four paws!" Billie pointed. "I see a nose, too. But how…?"

"The first paw points to our den," Grandpa said.

Billie Bear and Honeysuckle jumped for joy.

"Grandpa is so wise," Honeysuckle said. "I can't wait to tell Mama what he showed us!"

CHECK MY UNDERSTANDING

How does Grandpa solve the problem in the story?

_____

_____

_____

WRITE ABOUT IT Write what happens next! Use details from the story to write what Billie and Honeysuckle tell their mother when they get home. Draw a picture to go with your writing.

_____

_____

_____

_____

_____

_____

_____

_____

_____

_____

_____

Prepare to Read

GENRE STUDY **Poetry** uses images, sounds, and rhythm to express feelings. As you read *Water Rolls, Water Rises*, look for:

- alliteration, or a pattern of words with the same first sound (like *can* and *cats*)
- the line breaks in each stanza
- repetition of sounds, words, or lines
- words that appeal to the senses

SET A PURPOSE As you read, use the poet's words to **create mental images,** or make pictures in your mind. How do the pictures help you understand what the poet is describing?

POWER WORDS

strokes

tumbling

plumes

wisps

Meet Pat Mora.

Water Rolls, Water Rises

by Pat Mora   illustrated by Meilo So

*W*ater rolls
onto the shore
under the sun, under the moon.

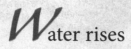 Water rises
into soft fog,
weaves down the street, strokes an old cat.

*B*lown by the wind,
water sails high.
Tumbling cloud plumes curl through the air.

Slow into rivers,
water slithers and snakes
through silent canyons at twilight and dawn.

Down smooth canals,
water streams, water slides,
gliding up roots of tulips and corn.

Filling deep wells,
water hums in the dark,
sloshes in buckets, quenches our thirst.

*S*wirling in wisps,
water twists then it twirls,
frosts scattered dry leaves, rubs lonely, bare trees.

In storms, water plunges
in thunder's brash roar,
races through branches from lightning's white flash.

*T*hen water rests,
drowsy in reservoirs,
its glistening silence shimmers like stars.

In the murmur of marsh wind,
water slumbers on moss,
whispers soft songs far under frog feet.

*W*ater burbles in springs,
gurgles and turns
down streams and rivers seeking the sea.

Skidding and slipping,
swooping round bends,
spinning on tree roots, careening down cliffs.

*L*ooping and leaping,
rushing to dive
into glimmering sea waves, spangle and splash.

Around our round world,
water rolls, water rises
under gold sun, under white moon.

Turn and Talk

Use details from *Water Rolls, Water Rises* to answer these questions with a partner.

1. **Create Mental Images** Close your eyes and picture one of the settings in the text. Describe what you see, hear, and smell. Which of the author's words help you create the picture?

2. Why do you think the author wrote this text? What does she want readers to know?

3. Why do you think this text uses illustrations instead of photographs to picture the author's words?

Talking Tip

Ask to learn more about one of your partner's ideas. Complete the sentence below.

Please explain _____.

Write a Poem

PROMPT How would you describe water in a poem? Find important details in the words and pictures from *Water Rolls, Water Rises* to help you explain your ideas.

PLAN First, make a details chart. On one side, write details about water. Then, think of interesting words that describe each detail. Write them on the other side of your chart.

Details	Words

WRITE Now write your poem using the best words from the chart. Remember to:

- Use words that paint a picture of your topic.

- Think about how the words in your poem sound together.

Water Rolls, Water Rises
by Pat Mora   Illustrated by Meilo So

_____

_____

_____

_____

_____

_____

_____

_____

_____

_____

Prepare to Read

GENRE STUDY **Poetry** uses images, sounds, and rhythm to express feelings.

MAKE A PREDICTION Preview "Matter Matters." What feelings might these two poems express? What might they be about?

_____

_____

_____

_____

_____

_____

SET A PURPOSE Read to see how poetry uses words in a special way to share information.

Matter Matters

READ In each line of the poem, look for words that begin with the same letter. Underline those words.

Some can be big, bumpy, or boxy.

Others can be small, sparkly, or squishy.

Let me give you a hint.

It is the kind of matter that

Does not change its

Shape! ▶

Close Reading Tip

Put a **?** by the parts you have questions about.

CHECK MY UNDERSTANDING

Why did the poet make the first letter of each line bold?

_____

_____

_____

READ Which of the poet's words help you to create a picture in your mind? <u>Underline</u> those words.

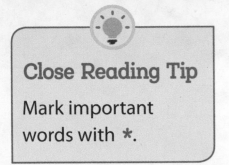
Liquids are everywhere,

In splashing seas and tiny teacups.

Quiet streams slowly slide,

Unless they freeze and turn to

Ice.

Don't slip!

CHECK MY UNDERSTANDING

What do you learn about matter from this poem? Use your own words to describe the poet's ideas.

_____

_____

_____

_____

_____

212

WRITE ABOUT IT   Write a poem like the poems in "Matter Matters." First, choose a state of matter. Write *SOLID, LIQUID*, or *GAS* in capital letters down the side of the paper. Next, write a sentence or phrase that begins with that letter on each line. What will your poem tell readers about that kind of matter?

_____

_____

_____

_____

_____

_____

_____

_____

_____

_____

_____

Prepare to Read

GENRE STUDY **Dramas** are plays that are read and performed. As you read *The Puddle Puzzle*, pay attention to:

- the cast of characters
- dialogue, or what the characters say
- setting, or where and when the story takes place
- stage directions that tell performers what to do

SET A PURPOSE **Ask questions** before, during, and after you read to help you get information or understand the text. Look for evidence in the text and pictures to **answer** your questions.

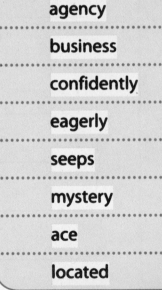

POWER WORDS

agency

business

confidently

eagerly

seeps

mystery

ace

located

Meet Ellen Weiss.

The Puddle Puzzle

by Ellen Weiss

illustrated by Joe Cepeda

Cast of Characters

TAYLOR

BRANDON

CARLOS

ADRIANA

Setting

a neighborhood on
a sunny spring day

Scene 1

TAYLOR: I am so excited! The Miller Detective Agency is open for business!

BRANDON: I am excited, too!

TAYLOR: Now we just have to wait for our first customer.

CARLOS: Is that the detective agency?

TAYLOR: Come over! We are open!

CARLOS: I am Carlos, and this is my sister Adriana. We have a problem.

TAYLOR: We are here to help! What is your problem?

CARLOS: Our puddle has vanished.

ADRIANA: We were playing in the puddle. Then the sun went away, so we went inside for lunch. When the sun came back out, we went outside to play again.

Miller

CARLOS: But our puddle was gone! Can you help us find it?

TAYLOR: This is a very hard case. We will do our best to solve it for you.

BRANDON: *(smiling confidently)* I know the answer! I know!

TAYLOR: Shhh, Brandon. I am the oldest, so I am in charge. We need to go and look for clues.

Scene 2

TAYLOR: This is where your puddle was located?

CARLOS: Yes, it was right here.

TAYLOR: *(taking out her notebook and writing)* One puddle, missing. *(She looks around.)* Maybe somebody stole it. Was anyone around here?

CARLOS: Nobody!

TAYLOR: Maybe it is hiding. I will look behind this bush. Nope! It is not here.

BRANDON: *(eagerly)* I know what happened!

TAYLOR: Shhh, Brandon!

BRANDON: But I know what happened!

TAYLOR: Now I am looking for footprints.

ADRIANA: Maybe we should let Brandon talk.

BRANDON: Thank you! Ahem. *(He clears his throat.)* A puddle is full of water, right?

CARLOS: Right!

BRANDON: But water can have three different forms.

CARLOS: It can?

BRANDON: Yes! When we are splashing in a puddle, the water is a liquid. If you freeze water, it turns into a solid.

ADRIANA: Ice!

BRANDON: There is one more thing water can be, too. It can be a gas.

ADRIANA: A gas?

BRANDON: Yes! When we boil water, the steam that seeps out of the kettle is a gas. When the sun shines on a puddle and heats it up, the water turns into a gas, too. A gas does not have a shape or a size. Sometimes we cannot even see it!

CARLOS: So that is what happened to our puddle!

BRANDON: It went into the air, and now we cannot see it or feel it. This is called evaporation.

TAYLOR: Mystery solved!

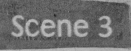

TAYLOR: Brandon, I'm sorry I didn't let you talk today. You knew the answer and I was too excited about gathering clues to listen. I think we need a new sign.

BRANDON: *(smiling proudly)* That is much better.

TAYLOR: We are ace detectives!

Miller & Miller
Science Detective
Agency

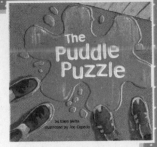

Use details from *The Puddle Puzzle* to answer these questions with a partner.

1. **Ask and Answer Questions** What questions did you ask yourself as Brandon and Taylor tried to solve the mystery? What questions did you ask at the end?

2. Which details explain what happened to the missing puddle?

3. How does the new sign make Brandon feel at the end of the drama? Why does he feel that way?

Talking Tip

Complete the sentence to add more to one of your partner's answers.

I'd like to add that _____.

Write Stage Directions

PROMPT Where would you add more stage directions to help readers perform the drama? Use details from the words and pictures to explain your answer.

PLAN First, draw a scene from the drama. Add labels that tell what the characters are doing or feeling.

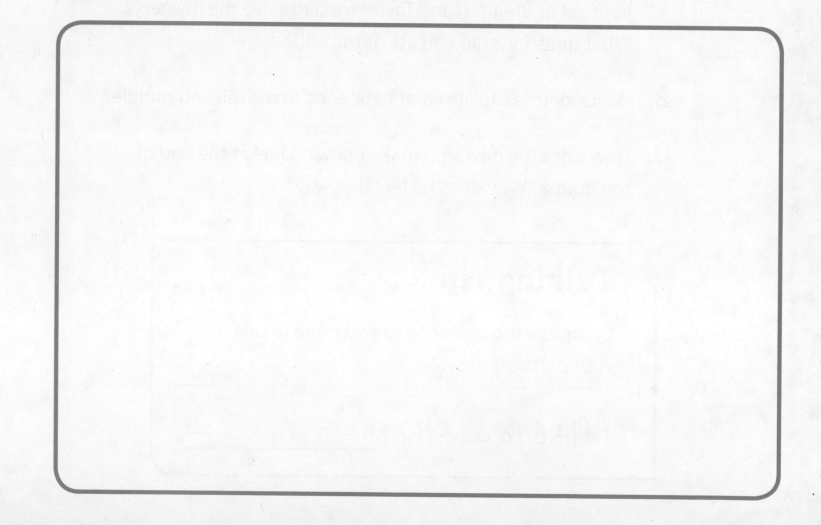

WRITE Now write stage directions you would like to add to the drama. Be sure they describe what the characters are doing or feeling as they say their lines. Remember to:

- Include words that clearly describe actions or feelings.

- Include the character's lines that the stage directions go with. Think about how you would read them.

The Puddle Puzzle

by Ellen Weiss
Illustrated by Joe Cepeda

_____

_____

_____

_____

_____

_____

_____

_____

Prepare to Read

GENRE STUDY **Dramas** are stories that are read and performed.

MAKE A PREDICTION Preview "Disappearing Daisies." Brandon and Taylor have a brand new case to solve. You know that dramas have characters, dialogue, and a setting. What do you think this drama will be about?

_____

_____

_____

_____

_____

_____

SET A PURPOSE Read to solve the case before Brandon and Taylor. As you read, ask yourself, "Is this an important clue?"

Disappearing Daisies

READ <u>Underline</u> the setting. Why is the setting important?

Cast of Characters: Brandon, Mom, Narrator, Taylor
Setting: the Miller home

MOM: I have a mystery to solve, kids. I need your help.

TAYLOR: Tell us the facts, and don't leave anything out.

MOM: Some daisies are missing from my flower garden. There are footprints all around the garden that are not mine.

NARRATOR: Brandon and Taylor looked at each other.

BRANDON: (*thoughtfully*) This is an interesting case. I think we can help.

TAYLOR: Yes, let's go dig up some clues in the flower garden. ▶

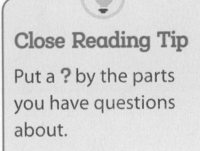

Close Reading Tip

Put a **?** by the parts you have questions about.

Close Reading Tip

Put a ! by a surprising part.

READ Look for a clue to help solve the mystery. <u>Underline</u> it.

NARRATOR: They went to the backyard to investigate.

BRANDON: When did you notice the flowers were missing?

MOM: Just a few minutes ago. They were here yesterday.

BRANDON: And is there anything special about this date?

TAYLOR: Yes, it's June 25th. Does that date mean anything to you?

MOM: *(looking surprised)* It's my birthday! I forgot all about it.

NARRATOR: Brandon and Taylor grinned. Brandon held out a big bouquet of daisies.

BRANDON and TAYLOR: Happy Birthday, Mom! We picked these for you!

MOM: You kids are the best detectives ever!

TAYLOR: Another case closed. Now, let's celebrate!

CHECK MY UNDERSTANDING

What questions did you ask yourself as you were trying to solve the mystery of the missing daisies?

_____

_____

WRITE ABOUT IT You used what you know about the
characters, dialogue, and setting to help you make predictions.
Did your predictions match what happened in the drama? Write
to tell what you were right about. Tell what happened differently.

_____

_____

_____

_____

_____

_____

_____

_____

_____

_____

Prepare to Read

GENRE STUDY **Fine art** describes art such as paintings, drawings, music, and dance. As you read *Looking at Art*, notice:

- people or objects in the art
- how the art makes you feel
- the subject of the art
- the type of artwork

SET A PURPOSE Look at what is happening in the art. Think about how it creates a story in your mind. Compare what you see in the art to what you read in the text.

Build Background: Art Critics

LOOKING AT ART

by Andrew Stevens

How does art imitate life? You learn things about the world around you every day. How can you do that with a painting? You can look at art for clues to help you understand what you see.

Jean Siméon Chardin painted *Soap Bubbles* around the year 1733. It shows a boy blowing a bubble. See his cheeks? If he were using big breaths, his cheeks would be puffed out. He must know the bubble will pop if it grows too quickly! The boy might be hoping the air will carry the bubble away.

If you lived in France long ago, you might see this scene in your neighborhood. What else can you figure out by studying the painting?

Jean Siméon Chardin,
Soap Bubbles
oil on canvas

Turn and Talk

Use details from *Looking at Art* and the painting *Soap Bubbles* to answer these questions with a partner.

1. **Connect Text and Visuals** What details from the image or the text tell you the painting was made a long time ago? How would it look different if the artist painted it today?

2. What are the characters doing in the painting? What do you think they will do next?

3. How does the author use words about science to tell about the painting?

Listening Tip

You learn from others by listening carefully. Think about what your partner says and what you learn.

Let's Wrap Up!

? Essential Question

How does exploring help us understand the world around us?

. . . .

Pick one of these activities to show what you have learned about the topic.

1. Observe, Explore, Discover!

You have read about how observing can help you learn about our world. Write five tips to help someone explore and make new discoveries. Look back at the texts for ideas about places and ways to explore.

Word Challenge

Can you use the word examine in your tips?

2. Picture the Matter

Draw or find pictures for each of the different kinds of matter. Then make a collage. Add labels to describe how the objects in your collage look, sound, feel, smell, or taste.

bouncy

round

My Notes

Glossary

A

ace [ās]   Someone described as ace is extremely good at something. He is an **ace** soccer player.

agency [ā'jən-sē]   If you work at an agency, your job is to help others to get something done. My neighbor works for a health **agency**.

amount [ə-mount']   An amount is how much there is of something. I would like a small **amount** of juice.

B

battleground [băt'l-ground']   A battleground is where a fight takes place. I visited the **battleground** where the war was won many years ago.

bellowed [běl'ōd]   If you bellowed, you shouted in a loud, deep voice. "Get away from there!" she **bellowed**.

blue [blo͞o]   When you feel blue, you feel sad. We are feeling **blue** today.

bounce [bouns]   When you bounce, you move up and down. I like to **bounce** my ball outside.

business [bĭz'nĭs]   A place open for business is ready to work, buy, or sell something. The coffee shop is now open for **business**.

C

citizen [sĭt'ĭ-zən]   A citizen is a member of a community, state, or country. I am a **citizen** of the United States.

compliment [kŏm'plə-mənt]   A compliment is a nice thing to say about someone. My teacher gave me a **compliment** about my work at school today.

confidently [kŏn'fĭ-dənt-lē]   When you do something confidently, you are sure you will do it well. She spoke **confidently** to the crowd.

cool [kōōl]   To cool how you feel means to calm down. Taking deep breaths helps me to **cool** down.

D

difference [dĭf'ər-əns, dĭf'rəns]   When people make a difference, they do something that helps others. Picking up litter helps us make a **difference** in the community.

disaster [dĭ-zăs'tər, dĭ-săs'tər]   A disaster is an event that goes horribly wrong. Leaving our dog alone with the new couch was a **disaster**, but we still love her.

E

eagerly [ē'gər-lē]   When you do something eagerly, you really want to do it. The student **eagerly** accepted her award.

easily [ē'zə-lē]   Something that is done easily is not hard to do. You can win the race **easily**.

elected [ĭ-lĕkt'ĭd]   Someone who is elected has been chosen for a job. My friend was **elected** to be class president.

examine [ĭg-zăm'ĭn]   When you examine something, you look at it carefully. We went outside to **examine** the footprints in the yard.

example [ĭg-zăm'pəl]   An example is a part of a larger group of things that are alike. This beautiful painting is one **example** of my favorite artist's work.

F

feud [fyōōd]   A feud is a long fight. My brother and I had a **feud** about sharing our toys.

fiddled [fĭd′ld]   If you fiddled with something, you kept touching it or playing with it. The girl **fiddled** with the zipper on her jacket.

forms [fôrmz]   Something with many forms has different shapes or ways of being. We are learning about the different **forms** of water in school today.

frenzy [frĕn′zē]   A frenzy is a time of great excitement and wild behavior. The big sale caused a shopping **frenzy**.

G

gasped [găspt]   If people gasped, they took a sharp breath in a surprised way. We **gasped** with surprise at the most exciting part.

grinned [grĭnd]   If you grinned, you smiled a wide smile. I **grinned** when I heard the happy news.

H

hamper [hăm′pər]   A hamper is a basket with a lid, used to hold dirty clothes. Please put your dirty clothes in the **hamper**.

handle [hăn′dl]   When you cannot handle something, you are not able to deal with it. I can **handle** doing more chores if I have some help.

I

identify [ī-dĕn′tə-fī′]   When you identify something, you say what it is. I want to **identify** the type of insect we found.

K

kind [kīnd]   Someone who is kind is nice, caring, or gentle. Helping others is one way to be **kind**.

L

local [lō′kəl]   Something that is local belongs to the area where you live. My mother works for the **local** newspaper.

located [lō'kāt'ĭd, lō-kāt'ĭd]   Where something is located is where it is. The map shows where the ponds are **located**.

M

material [mə-tîr'ē-əl]   Material is what something is made from. What **material** is that shirt made out of?

might [mīt]   Doing something with all your might is using all your power. He threw the ball with all his **might**.

mock [mŏk]   A mock version of something is not real. We set up a **mock** doctor's office for toys.

mood [mo͞od]   Your mood is the way you are feeling. I am in a great **mood** when I hear my favorite song.

munch [mŭnch]   When you munch food, you chew it loudly and completely. My friend likes to **munch** on carrots.

mystery [mĭs'tə-rē]   A mystery is something that is hard to understand or is not known about. The clues helped the detectives solve the **mystery**.

P

perfect [pûr'fĭkt]   When something is perfect, it is the best it can be. I felt proud of my **perfect** score on the quiz.

planet [plăn'ĭt]   A planet is a large object in space that moves around a star. Earth is the third **planet** from the sun.

planned [plănd]   If you planned, you decided ahead of time how you would do something. She **planned** to do her homework tomorrow.

plumes [plo͞omz]   Plumes are long, thin shapes that look like feathers. He saw **plumes** of smoke in the air.

proper [prŏp'ər]   Someone who is proper is polite and behaves well. It is **proper** to use your best manners at a tea party.

Q

queasy [kwē'zē]   If you are queasy, your stomach hurts and you feel sick. She knew she would feel **queasy** if she ate too much popcorn, so she just had a little bit.

R

realize [rē'ə-līz']   When you realize something, you know it or understand it. Do you **realize** that the event ends in an hour?

record [rĭ-kôrd']   When you record notes, you write them down. I like to **record** my story ideas in a notebook.

rough [rŭf]   When you do something in a rough way, you are not being gentle. Some sports can be too **rough** for children.

S

scowl [skoul]   A scowl is an angry frown. She had a **scowl** on her face after she heard the game was canceled.

seeps [sēps]   When something seeps, it passes slowly through a small opening. Honey **seeps** through a crack in the jar.

space [spās]   Space is an open area or place. The pool takes up a large **space** in the yard.

strokes [strōks]   When something strokes something else, it moves gently over that thing. My dog likes when my friend **strokes** her fur.

T

tasty [tā'stē]   Something that is tasty is good to eat. This salad dressing is so **tasty**.

tumbling [tŭm'blĭng]   Something that is tumbling is rolling over and over. We had fun **tumbling** across the lawn.

U

useful [yōōs'fəl]   Something that is useful is helpful. The book has many **useful** tips about camping.

W

wisps [wĭsps]   Wisps are thin streaks of something. I saw **wisps** of clouds in the sky.

Index of Titles and Authors

Acknowledgments

Excerpt from *Being a Good Citizen* (retitled from *Being a Good Citizen: A Kids' Guide to Community Involvement*) by Rachelle Kreisman, illustrated by Tim Haggerty. Copyright © 2016 by Red Chair Press LLC. Reprinted with the permission of Red Chair Press LLC.

Clark the Shark by Bruce Hale, illustrated by Guy Francis. Text copyright © 2013 by Bruce Hale. Illustrations copyright © 2013 by Guy Francis. Reprinted by permission of HarperCollins Publishers.

The Great Fuzz Frenzy by Janet Stevens and Susan Stevens Crummel. Text copyright © 2005 by Janet Stevens and Susan Stevens Crummel. Illustrations copyright © 2005 by Janet Stevens. Reprinted by permission of Houghton Mifflin Harcourt Publishing Company.

Excerpt from *Many Kinds of Matter* (retitled from *Many Kinds of Matter: A Look at Solids, Liquids, and Gases*) by Jennifer Boothroyd. Text copyright © 2011 by Lerner Publishing Group, Inc. Reprinted with the permission of Lerner Publishing Company, a division of Lerner Publishing Group, Inc.

Picture Day Perfection by Deborah Diesen, illustrated by Dan Santat. Text copyright © 2013 by Deborah Diesen. Illustrations copyright © 2013 by Dan Santat. Reprinted by permission of Express Permissions on behalf of Abrams Books for Young Readers, an imprint of Harry N. Abrams, Inc., New York and Trident Media Group, LLC.

Excerpt by Christopher Reeve from http://www.spinalcordinjury-paralysis.org/blogs/16/1784. Text copyright © by Christopher Reeve. Reprinted by permission of the Estate of Christopher Reeve.

Spoon by Amy Krouse Rosenthal, illustrated by Scott Magoon. Text copyright © 2009 by Amy Krouse Rosenthal. Illustrations copyright © 2009 by Scott Magoon. Reprinted by permission of Hyperion Books for Children, an imprint of Disney Publishing Group.

Water Rolls, Water Rises/El agua rueda, el agua sube by Pat Mora, illustrated by Meilo So. Text copyright © 2014 by Pat Mora. Illustrations copyright © 2014 by Meilo So. Reprinted by permission of Children's Book Press, an imprint of Lee & Low Books Inc.

Credits